THE
SHACK

A FIVE-WEEK STUDY ON LOVE, FORGIVENESS,
AND CONNECTING WITH GOD

OUTRE CH®

The Shack Study Guide

© 2017 by Outreach, Inc.

Published by Outreach, Inc., Colorado Springs, CO 80919

www.Outreach.com

ISBN: 9781635101331

Cover Design by Tim Downs

Interior Design by Alexia Garaventa

Written by Jeremy Jones

Printed in the United States of America

CONTENTS

INTRODUCTION

Welcome to *The Shack Study Guide,* your five-week guide to the biblical themes and lessons drawn from the highly anticipated feature film *The Shack.*

Based on *The New York Times* best-selling novel, *The Shack* takes us on a father's uplifting spiritual journey. After suffering a family tragedy, Mack Phillips (played by Sam Worthington) spirals into a deep depression, causing him to question his innermost beliefs. Facing a crisis of faith, he receives a mysterious letter urging him to come to an abandoned shack deep in the Oregon wilderness. Despite his doubts, Mack journeys to the shack and encounters an enigmatic trio of strangers—all three persons of the Trinity—led by a woman named Papa (played by Octavia Spencer). Through this meeting, Mack finds important truths that will transform his understanding of his tragedy and change his life forever.

In many ways, *The Shack* is a modern-day parable, similar to the stories Jesus told to help people better understand the truth He wanted to communicate. *The Shack* is an artistic and imaginative representation of a deeply personal story that explores encountering God's love. It raises provocative questions and points us toward the path for healing out of impossible tragedy. For all those who have wondered where God is in their pain, for those who have questioned if God is there at all, *The Shack* presents an unforgettable encounter with a divine love that promises to never leave us.

The story of *The Shack* applies to us all, whether we have endured terrible tragedy and pain or the more common struggles of everyday life. The movie and this study guide are honest, applicable, and accessible whether you are looking for faith, have lost faith along the way, or are strong in your faith but desire to trust God more deeply. Wherever you find yourself on your spiritual journey, welcome to *The Shack Study Guide*, a place to wrestle with your questions, start a conversation, and explore the answers with God.

A NOTE ABOUT PAPA

One notable feature of the film that might catch viewers by surprise is the depiction of God. Papa is a woman. Jesus is a young carpenter of Middle Eastern descent. Sarayu, the Holy Spirit, is in the form of an Asian woman. These characters are not meant as literal portrayals of God or as a theological statement on the gender or race of God. Instead, they are an artistic way of presenting the different aspects of God's character in each member of the Trinity. They are creative representations of God's transcendence and goodness. God is above and beyond all earthly limitations, and in His goodness, He desires to break down all boundaries in order to reach us with His compassion and saving grace in a way we can understand and relate to.

That's what we see Him doing with Mack. In the context of the story, Mack has rejected God in the past, but God is reaching out to him. Early in the movie, we see that Mack and his mother were abused by his alcoholic father. This naturally shapes Mack's view of God as a father and is a big part of why Mack rejects God. And as we'll hear Papa tell him, "After what you've been through, I didn't think you could handle a father right now." Papa knows what Mack needs and longs to heal him, and Papa reaches out to Mack in a representation he can relate to. It brings to mind the way Isaiah described God comforting Israel like a mother: "As a mother comforts her child, so will I comfort you; and you will be comforted over Jerusalem" (Isaiah 66:13).

It feels a bit like Aslan, the great lion in *The Chronicles of Narnia*. On first hearing that the true king of Narnia is a lion rather than a man, one of the main characters, Susan, responds, "Ooh, I'd thought he was a man. Is he quite safe? I shall feel rather nervous about meeting a lion." Her host, Mr. Beaver, replies, "Safe? Who said anything about safe? 'Course he isn't safe. But he's good."[1]

C. S. Lewis wasn't teaching that God is a lion. And *The Shack* isn't teaching that God is a woman. What we find in both are beautiful depictions of God's character and His relentless love and pursuit of each of us walking in the earthly constraints and brokenness of this human life.

God is in the business of disintegrating our assumptions and expectations and replacing them with an invitation to trust His goodness as He works in our lives. He will stop at nothing to draw us closer and demonstrate His love to us. We even see later in the film that Papa appears as a man and tells Mack that a father figure is what's needed for the challenge Mack has to face at that time. In much deeper ways than gender, God is not at all who or what Mack expected.

---

1 C. S. Lewis, *The Lion, the Witch and the Wardrobe* (New York: HarperCollins, 1950), 79–80.

HOW TO USE THIS STUDY GUIDE

Based on the movie *The Shack,* this study guide is designed to help viewers raise big questions and wrestle through them in light of God's Word. Maybe they are questions you've already had. Maybe they are questions you were afraid to ask. Using powerful scenes from the film, paired with relevant Scripture, this study is an invitation to embark on an encounter with God. Ultimately, only you can answer life's big questions for yourself. Hopefully *The Shack* and this study can offer a compelling story and guide to help frame some of those questions and open the dialogue inside.

This book is designed primarily as a five-week study guide that can be used by small groups, Sunday school classes, or Bible study groups. However, it can also be used by individuals, and it makes a great follow-up gift for visitors who attend a movie event.

The following sections are found in each of the five chapters in this book:

FOCUS

The key verse (or verses) represents the main theme of the study and provides a way to focus on the central message. The focus verses are an excellent opportunity for Scripture memorization if any group members choose to do so.

WATCH

Each lesson connects to a relevant scene from the movie *The Shack*. A short Setup description sets the stage for the scene and offers a bit of background info and a brief overview. This can be helpful to read before watching the video clip.

DISCUSS

The main course of the study, this section leads with discussion questions, raises supporting Scripture, and offers brief insights to guide group discussion and personal reflection. In a group setting, responses to the questions should open dialogue and offer greater breadth and depth of application for all.

ABIDE

This written prayer can be the launching point for an individual's personal time of prayer. It can also be used in a group setting. Read it aloud as a group, or use it as the beginning or end of a prayer time where group members are encouraged to speak their own prayers.

TAKE IT WITH YOU

These final questions are meant to be explored personally and followed up during the week between small group sessions. They can provide personal reflection and a framework for journaling about what you are studying and learning.

PRACTICE

This section offers a challenge and suggested action for application. The Message of the Week is an encouraging quote from the movie; think of it as a message from God to you. Next is a recommended hands-on, active way for each individual to respond to what they are learning and to carry the lesson into the flow of their week. Consider it a type of homework assignment for group members. Encourage your group members to share with each other what they did during the previous week, how it went, and how it impacted their journeys of trusting God.

INFO BOXES

Throughout each lesson you will find content that is pulled out and highlighted in information boxes. These include Bible verses, quotes from the movie, quotes from the actors and actresses in the movie, and other engaging tidbits. These can be used simply as interesting supplemental information or as a launching point for further discussion, reflection, inspiration, and discovery.

WHERE IS GOD WHEN I NEED HIM THE MOST?

FOCUS

"All this is from God, who reconciled us to himself through Christ and gave us the ministry of reconciliation: that God was reconciling the world to himself in Christ, not counting people's sins against them."
—2 Corinthians 5:18–19

WATCH

Setup: Following the heart-wrenching tragedy of losing his youngest daughter and the deep suffering of depression—"the Great Sadness"—that has overtaken Mack, he has finally made his way back to the epicenter of his deepest pain. But inside the shack, Mack has found a very different place than he expected. And he encounters God in ways he never dreamed.

Leading up to this scene, Mack has already met all three persons of the Trinity. And God is nothing like Mack expected. As he is still trying to make sense of it all, he enters the kitchen and begins to have his first real conversation with Papa. Papa hands Mack a mass of dough and shows him how to work it. As they knead dough side by side, it doesn't take long to get to the root of Mack's pain.

 Watch Video 1: Where Is God?

DISCUSS

Don't Hold Back

Knowing how Mack got to this place and time, what are the emotions you think he's feeling? Can you relate to Mack? Why or why not?

What is the main theme of Mack's first real discussion with Papa?

> "I KNOW WHAT A GREAT GULF THERE IS BETWEEN US. YOU MAY NOT BELIEVE IT, BUT I AM ESPECIALLY FOND OF YOU."
>
> —PAPA

Do you think Mack is being fair in this conversation? Is Papa? Why or why not?

What would you say if you had a chance to talk to God face-to-face?

Is it okay to ask God your hardest, most troubling questions? Why or why not?

Have you ever done so? Did it hurt or help you? In what ways?

What do we do with pain? How do we handle the hurt? Especially when it comes from the worst this life on earth can offer: tragedy, injustice, abuse, disease, you name it. You may not have experienced the loss of a child like Mack, but we all have painful experiences. We all feel the weight of a broken world. And at the heart of it all lie the questions: How can I know that God is good when everything feels like He isn't? How can I know God is there when all I feel is abandoned?

These are undoubtedly big questions. They are universal. They've been grappled with by experts and average Joes, so we won't come up with the ultimate be-all, end-all answer in our short discussion. But let's look at some starting points that can offer encouragement and hope.

First, God can handle our questions. We don't have to hold back with Him. He understands our emotions. He knows our thoughts and feelings whether we give voice to them or not. And He hurts with our hurts. He is with us in the pain.

David, arguably Israel's greatest king, offers us excellent examples in his psalms. He wasn't afraid to tell God exactly what he was feeling. Consider these examples:

> How long, LORD? Will you forget me forever?
>> How long will you hide your face
>> from me?
> How long must I wrestle with my thoughts
>> and day after day have sorrow in my heart?
> How long will my enemy triumph over me?
> (Psalm 13:1–2)

> My God, my God, why have you forsaken me?
>> Why are you so far from saving me,
>> so far from my cries of anguish?
> My God, I cry out by day, but you do not answer,
>> by night, but I find no rest. (Psalm 22:1–2)

> "THE REAL UNDERLYING FLAW IN YOUR LIFE IS THAT YOU DON'T THINK THAT I AM GOOD."
>
> —PAPA

Did God get angry at David for his honest outbursts? This is how God described David much later in history and in the Bible—even after David's failures, including the Bathsheba affair and its murderous cover-up: "After removing Saul, he made David their king. God testified concerning him: 'I have found David son of Jesse, a man after my own heart; he will do everything I want him to do'" (Acts 13:22).

Surprising? David's relationship with God was marked by honesty. It's the same kind of transparency Papa welcomes from Mack.

God Meets Us

Why do you think Papa appears to Mack as an African American woman in their early encounters?

> "DON'T EVER THINK THAT WHAT MY
> SON CHOSE TO DO DIDN'T COST US
> BOTH DEARLY."
> —PAPA

If God were to appear to you in human form, who would He be based on in your current perception of God? Who would be the most approachable and comforting persona? Who would most defy your stereotypes of God?

What personifications of God the Father, Son, and Holy Spirit would you expect if you were in Mack's shoes? Do the movie portrayals encourage or bother you? Why?

In the movie, how did God the Father, Son, and Holy Spirit meet Mack where he was in his level of understanding and need? How did they each also challenge his perceptions and draw him into deeper relationship?

God's love drives Him to do whatever it takes to get through to us. What an example of how God transcends earthly limitations in order to meet with us in meaningful ways when Papa takes the earthly form of an African American woman cooking in the kitchen! Because of the history of abuse in Mack's past by his human father, Papa knows that Mack can't handle a father figure at this point in his journey. So Papa allows Mack to encounter love and goodness in another form—one from a person in his past who offered a true example of God's love, one that can still help convey love and acceptance to Mack.

Sure, this is a fictional portrayal. But we can draw encouragement from it that God ignores our narrow concepts of Him and intersects us in our need, driven by goodness, love, and compassion. God knows our needs, and He is willing to do what it takes to reach us there.

> "THERE WAS SOMETHING ABOUT THIS PROJECT THAT I FEEL THE WORLD NEEDS. IT'S A BALM. IT JUST CREATED THIS CALM FOR ME IN MY LIFE, AND THERE'S JUST SO MUCH LIGHT AROUND IT."
>
> —OCTAVIA SPENCER, WHO PLAYS PAPA

God is in the business of disintegrating our assumptions and expectations and replacing them with an invitation to encounter His love and allow Him to work in our lives. God is not hiding from us. He is pursuing us, and He will stop at nothing to draw us closer and demonstrate His love to us.

What examples do you remember from the Bible of God using various forms to represent His presence or to speak to someone? (Hint: Think burning bush, pillar of cloud and of fire, angels, a donkey.)

Was Jesus who or what the people expected of the Messiah? In what ways did He challenge or shatter their preconceived ideas?

Read and discuss the following Bible verses. How do they encourage you about encountering God?

> Come near to God and he will come near to you. (James 4:8)

> Ask and it will be given to you; seek and you will find; knock and the door will be opened to you. For everyone who asks receives; the one who seeks finds; and to the one who knocks, the door will be opened. (Matthew 7:7–8)

> I do believe; help me overcome my unbelief! (Mark 9:24)

What does it look like to believe and act upon these verses?

God Was There—God Is Here

Is there something Mack is missing in his outlook about pain?

As Mack and Papa continue to talk, Papa reveals scars on her wrists. Why do they matter? What's the significance?

How does the Trinity relate to the cross? Why is it important?

> "TASTE AND SEE THAT THE LORD IS GOOD; BLESSED IS THE ONE WHO TAKES REFUGE IN HIM."
>
> —PSALM 34:8

We often look at the horror of the *what* of the cross but lose sight of the powerful *why*: the heart of God. Unfortunately, we see the penalty and the judgment and an angry God whose wrath must be appeased. And whether we admit it or not, we view Jesus as a nice God but His Dad as a God with anger management issues. We may not say it out loud, but we find ourselves feeling kind of like Mack: If salvation is found by God somehow beating up His best kid and hanging Him out to suffer on His own, why in the world would I want anything to do with the Father? It's a viewpoint that sees God as the ultimate punisher and angry judge.

We're not sure exactly what Mack believes about God, but it seems clear that he feels like God is the ultimate punisher with a terrible habit of abandoning people when they need Him most. But maybe Mack isn't seeing everything correctly. Maybe his perspective is incomplete. Maybe seeing God's Trinity as a

> "I WANT TO HEAL THAT WOUND
> THAT HAS GROWN INSIDE YOU,
> AND BETWEEN US."
> —PAPA

"good cop, bad cop" arrangement is wrong. Where can we find hope for a better explanation?

Deeper insight comes from the apostle Paul in 2 Corinthians 5:18–19: "All this is from God, who reconciled us to himself through Christ and gave us the ministry of reconciliation: that God was reconciling the world to himself in Christ, not counting people's sins against them."

God as Trinity, as three beings in one God, is a mind-bending concept that exists outside the normal confines of our physical world. Seeing three different characters in the movie is a helpful personification, and their interplay offers many interesting, even funny, insights. But maybe what's most important for us to grasp emotionally about the Trinity is that God is a living community of love and a unified presence.

When Jesus suffered on the cross, God was there, "reconciling the world to himself in Christ." Jesus told His disciples, "Anyone who has seen me has seen the

Father" (John 14:9). When Jesus cried out, "My God, my God, why have you forsaken me?" (Matthew 27:46), it was His human form blinded by the sin of the whole world. God was with Him.

Think of how you create a cure for a snakebite by bringing forth an anti-venom. You find a host that somehow possesses in its blood an antibody that is more powerful than the poison. When you introduce the poison into that host, an antidote can be manufactured in the process. That antidote can be given to everyone who is inflicted with the disease—it is a cure.

That is what happened on the cross. That is what Jesus, the Father, and the Holy Spirit did in the laboratory of time and space in the spirit realm of that moment. They did much more than inflict and endure punishment to satisfy some judicial decree. They produced a cure for the disease of sin.

Why? So God could heal us.

Read and discuss the following Bible verses. What hope do they offer?

> As a mother comforts her child,
> > so will I comfort you;
> > and you will be comforted over Jeru-
> > salem. (Isaiah 66:13)

> The LORD himself goes before you and
> will be with you; he will never leave you

> "THE LORD IS GRACIOUS AND COMPASSIONATE, SLOW TO ANGER AND RICH IN LOVE. THE LORD IS GOOD TO ALL; HE HAS COMPASSION ON ALL HE HAS MADE."
>
> —PSALM 145:8–9

nor forsake you. Do not be afraid; do not be discouraged. (Deuteronomy 31:8)

In the same way, the Spirit helps us in our weakness. We do not know what we ought to pray for, but the Spirit himself intercedes for us through wordless groans. And he who searches our hearts knows the mind of the Spirit, because the Spirit intercedes for God's people in accordance with the will of God. (Romans 8:26–27)

ABIDE

God, thank you that, at the core of your being, you are good and you show your love and goodness to us in so many ways. Please meet us in our pain and show us that you are bigger than our hurt. Please help us to trust you as we look for you through the hard moments of life. And please guide us deeper into your truth, which you promise will set us free.

TAKE IT WITH YOU

What great question is defining your life? How does it shape and guide your everyday thoughts, attitudes, and actions?

PRACTICE

Message of the Week: "I am especially fond of you."

Memory Stones: Throughout the Old Testament, we see examples of God's people creating physical reminders of God's love, goodness, and faithfulness. One example is the altar built by the Israelites after the waters of the Jordan River parted to allow them to cross into the Promised Land. At Joshua's command, each of the twelve tribes took a stone from the river, and Joshua used them to build an altar to God. Joshua 4:20–24 says,

> And Joshua set up at Gilgal the twelve stones they had taken out of the Jordan. He said to the Israelites, "In the future when your descendants ask their parents, 'What do these stones mean?' tell them, 'Israel crossed the Jordan on dry ground.' For the LORD your God dried up the Jordan before you until you had crossed over. The LORD your God did to the Jordan what he had done to the Red Sea when he dried it up before us until we had crossed over. He did this so that

> "WHEN ALL YOU SEE IS YOUR PAIN,
> YOU LOSE SIGHT OF ME."
> —PAPA

all the peoples of the earth might know that the hand of the LORD is powerful and so that you might always fear the LORD your God."

We are often like the Israelites—quick to forget and in need of clear reminders of God's goodness. So this week, practice the experience of the memory stones.

Select a small stone and carry it in your pocket. Each time you feel it in your pocket or take it out to look at, repeat Papa's message to yourself: "I am especially fond of you."

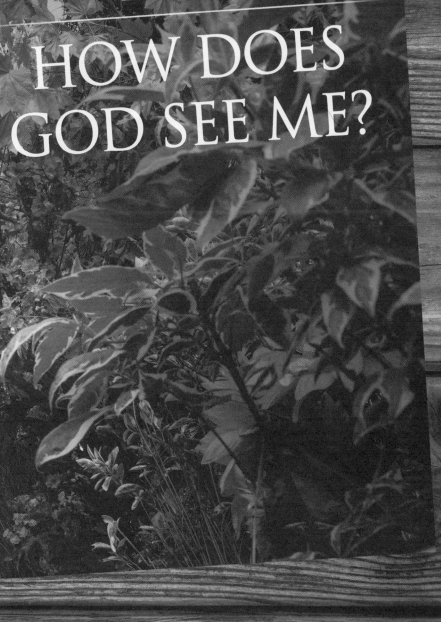

LESSON 2

HOW DOES GOD SEE ME?

FOCUS

"And we know that in all things God works for the good of those who love him, who have been called according to his purpose." —Romans 8:28

WATCH

Setup: Mack has another conversation with Papa. "As difficult as it is for you to accept, I am in the middle of everything you perceive to be a mess, working for your good," Papa says. "That's what I do." But Mack isn't buying it. The way he sees it, Papa didn't do any good by not saving his daughter, and he lashes out to let Papa know. It seems Mack has had enough of the shack—and Papa. He storms into the forest looking for the way out. Instead, he encounters Sarayu.

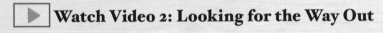 **Watch Video 2: Looking for the Way Out**

DISCUSS

I Am the Mess

Mack has the chance to leave if he wants to. Why does he stay?

In what ways do we look for the way out from what God wants to work within us?

"YOU WEREN'T MEANT TO DO ANY OF THAT ALL ON YOUR OWN. THAT WAS THE LIE IN THE FIRST GARDEN. THIS WAS ALWAYS MEANT TO BE THE FRUIT OF A RELATIONSHIP. A CONVERSATION BETWEEN FRIENDS."

—SARAYU

What is significant about Sarayu telling Mack, "We're not trying to justify anything. We'd like to heal it—if you let us"?

What's the difference between justifying pain and healing pain?

What is it that Sarayu wants help with in the garden?

What do we look like on the inside? No, we're not being figurative here—yet, anyway. Have you ever seen inside a human body, maybe in a science class or surgery video? There's a lot of blood and guts crammed inside our skin. It's messy, gross, oozy, and bloody—but it's all oh-so incredibly complex and amazing! The intricacies and abilities of the human body are incredible. It's beautiful.

Now let's talk metaphorically. What do we look like inside emotionally? Spiritually? If you were going to paint a picture of that scene for yourself, what kind of shapes and colors would you use?

This is the part of us that we often don't want to reveal to others, to God, or even to ourselves. We'd rather reflect and deflect people's attention with the shell of our exterior. That way, we can keep them out. We can mask our insecurities, hide our fears, or avoid our pain.

Many of us try to do the same with God. We try to hold Him at arm's length, to only let Him get so close. Reasons vary, but often they're rooted in fear, mistrust, and shame. We don't want to let God in because we're afraid of what He might find there. Maybe we're afraid He'll be angry or punish us for the darkness lurking inside our hearts. Maybe we're afraid He can't really help or do anything about the hurt weighing us down inside. Maybe we're mad at Him, blaming Him for the pain we've experienced. Maybe it's a little bit of everything.

We can be a lot like Adam and Eve in Genesis 3:8–10: "Then the man and his wife heard the sound of the

Lord God as he was walking in the garden in the cool of the day, and they hid from the Lord God among the trees of the garden. But the Lord God called to the man, 'Where are you?' He answered, 'I heard you in the garden, and I was afraid because I was naked; so I hid.'"

But is it possible our perspective is wrong? Could it be that God sees beauty in our mess?

A Different View?

Compare and contrast Genesis 3:8–10 with Genesis 1:27–28, 31: "So God created mankind in his own image, in the image of God he created them; male and female he created them. God blessed them. . . . God saw all that he had made, and it was very good." What differences or similarities do you see?

How did God view Adam and Eve? What was God's original relationship with them like?

"[THE FILM] IS POWERFUL, AND IT REALLY JUST OPENS YOUR WORLD AND MAKES YOU THINK OF HOW BEAUTIFUL THIS WORLD REALLY IS AND CAN BE. IT GIVES US A LOT OF HOPE."

—SUMIRE MATSUBARA, WHO PLAYS SARAYU

Mack sees the garden as a mess. "Isn't it beautiful?" Sarayu says. What do you think made this wild place beautiful to Sarayu?

What words do you think God would use to describe you?

> "IT'S NOT THE WORK, BUT THE PURPOSE THAT MAKES IT SPECIAL."
> —SARAYU

Let's see what the Bible says about God's view of us. Read and discuss the following verses. What do they say about how God sees you?

> For you created my inmost being;
>   you knit me together in my mother's womb.
> I praise you because I am fearfully and wonderfully made;
>   your works are wonderful. . . .
> How precious to me are your thoughts, God!
>   How vast is the sum of them! (Psalm 139:13–14, 17)

> Since you are precious and honored in my sight,
>   and because I love you,
> I will give people in exchange for you,
>   nations in exchange for your life.
>   (Isaiah 43:4)

> Are not five sparrows sold for two pennies?
> Yet not one of them is forgotten by God.
> Indeed, the very hairs of your head are all

numbered. Don't be afraid; you are worth more than many sparrows. (Luke 12:6–7)

For we are God's handiwork, created in Christ Jesus to do good works, which God prepared in advance for us to do. (Ephesians 2:10)

See what great love the Father has lavished on us, that we should be called children of God! And that is what we are! (1 John 3:1)

Therefore, if anyone is in Christ, the new creation has come: The old has gone, the new is here! (2 Corinthians 5:17)

Abiding in Christ

In Eden, Adam and Eve bought the lie from the serpent that "your eyes will be opened, and you will be like God, knowing good and evil" (Genesis 3:5). At its core, the lie claimed that they didn't need God. They could be like God. They could do it all on their own.

Sarayu brings up this point when she and Mack are talking in the garden about discerning good from evil. "You weren't meant to do any of that all on your own," she says. "This was always meant to be the fruit of a relationship—a conversation between friends."

Adam and Eve originally had that organic conversation with God, walking and talking with Him face-to-face, without shame. Mack is being offered a taste of it. We can experience it too—if we want. It's a voluntary give-and-take. The connection and conversation are offered to all, but we're faced with a choice daily, hourly, by the minute. Will we choose to take on life independent and separate from God? Or will we choose dependence and dialogue, allowing God to lead?

What does it look like for us to have a "conversation between friends" with God?

What keeps us from this kind of intimate dialogue with God? What role does fear play?

> "WILD AND WONDERFUL,
> AND PERFECTLY IN PROCESS.
> MAGNIFICENT!"
> —SARAYU

What are Mack and Sarayu working on in the garden?
Why is it important that they work together?

What can Sarayu see about this place that Mack cannot? How does it change the whole process and setting?

PAUL YOUNG, AUTHOR OF THE BEST-SELLING BOOK *THE SHACK*, STARTED WRITING THE STORY AS A CHRISTMAS GIFT FOR HIS CHILDREN. AS HE DEVELOPED THE CHARACTERS, HE WAS SEARCHING FOR A NAME FOR THE HOLY SPIRIT. WHILE ON A SKYPE CALL AT WORK WITH A WOMAN FROM INDIA, HE ASKED HER TO GIVE HIM ALL THE NAMES FOR WIND IN HER DIALECT. *SARAYU* WAS ONE THAT CAUGHT HIS ATTENTION. WHEN HE ASKED THE WOMAN WHAT KIND OF WIND THIS WAS, SHE REPLIED, "WELL, *SARAYU* IS THE COMMON WIND THAT CATCHES YOU BY SURPRISE." AND SO SARAYU IT WAS.

Jesus offered us a beautiful garden metaphor in John 15:

> I am the true vine, and my Father is the gardener. He cuts off every branch in me that bears no fruit, while every branch that does bear fruit he prunes so that it will be even more fruitful. You are already clean because of the word I have spoken to you. Remain in me, as I also remain in you. No branch can bear fruit by itself; it must remain in the vine. Neither can you bear fruit unless you remain in me. (verses 1–4)

We often view pruning as a painful process. We think of the cutting aspect. But in the context Jesus was using, does it hurt to cut off a dead branch? There is certainly a removal, but it is a clearing out of old, withered remains to make room for new growth. Pruning may be painful sometimes, but not always. To use a more personal example, think about your hair and fingernails. We cut our hair and trim our fingernails regularly without pain to allow them to grow more healthily. It's a process.

Similarly, Jesus was talking about a process: remaining, abiding in Him, drawing nutrients and sustenance and life from Him so that fruit can naturally grow out of us. Perhaps our view of the process comes back to the question of how we view the gardener: Can I trust Him? Is He really there for me? Is His love truly good? Does He really find me beautiful, mess and all?

What's your perception of the pruning process Jesus described?

Is God a gardener who can be trusted? Why or why not?

What does this garden in *The Shack* represent?

How can you enter the conversation and process with God this week, in the midst of whatever life is bringing you?

"AND WE KNOW THAT IN ALL THINGS GOD WORKS FOR THE GOOD OF THOSE WHO LOVE HIM, WHO HAVE BEEN CALLED ACCORDING TO HIS PURPOSE."

—ROMANS 8:28

ABIDE

God, thank you that your Holy Spirit is constantly at work in our lives to transform what we see as a mess into a beautiful picture of your love and grace. Help us to grow in our trust in you and in your purpose for us. Give us the strength, courage, and patience to obey your instructions, even when we don't understand.

TAKE IT WITH YOU

What are you looking for the way out of? Where in your life is God drawing you to regeneration and a new conversation between friends?

PRACTICE

Message of the Week: "Wild and wonderful, and perfectly in process. Magnificent!"

Perspective Walk: Plan a time to take a slow walk this week. While you walk, be intentional about watching for things that look different from different perspectives. Maybe it's the water in a puddle, which looks like a lake up close but a small puddle from a distance. Maybe it's a group of flowers, which looks like a beautiful garden up close, but a longer perspective reveals they are growing in a small crack in the concrete. Perhaps it's a blazing sun, which fades into a soft sunset over the span of a few minutes. Or even the up-close design of something (like a tire tread) that is hard to identify until you see the whole thing.

When you find something that catches your attention, take two pictures that represent different perspectives of the same object. Save the photos on your phone, and review them throughout the week. Set one of them as your phone's background image where you can see it often. Or print and frame the pair side by side as a reminder to trust God's purpose and His wider perspective as He is at work in your life. Write this caption on or near your photos as a reminder of your own life: "Wild and wonderful, and perfectly in process. Magnificent!"

LESSON 3

WHY ARE YOU DOING THIS TO ME?

FOCUS

"God has said, 'Never will I leave you; never will I forsake you.'" —Hebrews 13:5

WATCH

Setup: After Mack leaves the garden, he encounters Jesus at the workshop. Talking with Jesus is much more comfortable for Mack. So when Jesus invites him to see something on the other side of the lake, Mack relents—at least after Jesus tells him he can take the boat and fish his way over. Jesus will catch up soon. With a little encouragement, Mack boards the rowboat and sets out across the beautiful waters. As Mack dips his oars, he actually begins to relax—but not for long.

▶ **Watch Video 3: Trust Me**

DISCUSS

Left to Ourselves

Why does Jesus send Mack out on the boat?

What happens when Mack is left to himself?

What do you think the boat represents?

"Why are you doing this to me?" Mack says. Is it blame, or is it a sincere question? Explain.

What does Jesus mean when He tells Mack, "This is happening inside you. You're letting it consume you, and you don't have to"?

"Why are you doing this to me?" Mack's words come quickly, almost immediately. They seem to be his default response. As we watch the movie unfold and see what Mack has gone through, we can't help but feel for him.

As we watch him struggle, it's easy to understand how he could doubt God and even blame God. We can see why he's hurt and angry. God hasn't kept Mack free from abuse. He hasn't stopped the harm to Mack's daughter. He hasn't removed the pain or

> "I KEEP MY EYES ALWAYS ON THE LORD. WITH HIM AT MY RIGHT HAND, I WILL NOT BE SHAKEN."
> —PSALM 16:8

the Great Sadness from Mack's life. But this scene on the water gives us new insight into how these events are continuing to haunt Mack—and how he can break free of them.

Look at Me

How are Mack and Jesus viewing this experience differently? Compare and contrast their words.

Have you ever been riding a bike and looked ahead to see a pothole or rock in the middle of the road or trail? The natural thing is to look at it, but the longer you look at it, the more likely you are to steer right toward it. Even if the intent of your focus is to avoid something in the way, focusing on it often causes you to head directly toward it. Similarly, when Mack looks at the rising water, it becomes more powerful and sucks him in.

You've probably been in a similar place at some point or another. None of us is immune to difficulty, hardship, or pain. When we focus on our circumstances, or on the pain inside ourselves, we are easily overwhelmed. But when we encounter pain—whether memories rising from our past or struggles unfolding in the everyday present—we are faced with a choice. What will we allow our minds to dwell on?

We can blame God and allow our hurt to overwhelm us. Or we can look to God and listen to His voice. We can choose to remain on our own and drown in our sorrow and fear. Or we can take our cues from God.

What is the antidote in that moment of choice? "Look at Me," Jesus says. "Listen to My voice." When we turn our focus to Jesus, we can hear and respond to His guidance. We can breathe with Him.

What does God's voice tell us? Read and discuss the following Bible verses.

> And be sure of this: I am with you always, even to the end of the age. (Matthew 28:20, NLT)

> I have told you these things, so that in me you may have peace. In this world you

will have trouble. But take heart! I have overcome the world. (John 16:33)

Peace I leave with you; my peace I give you. I do not give to you as the world gives. Do not let your hearts be troubled and do not be afraid. (John 14:27)

We do this by keeping our eyes on Jesus, the champion who initiates and perfects our faith. Because of the joy awaiting him, he endured the cross, disregarding its shame. Now he is seated in the place of honor beside God's throne. (Hebrews 12:2, NLT)

"MACK! THIS IS HAPPENING INSIDE YOU. YOU'RE LETTING IT CONSUME YOU, AND YOU DON'T HAVE TO. JUST TAKE A DEEP BREATH, AND LISTEN TO MY VOICE."
—JESUS

Into the Miracle

What happens next in *The Shack?* Mack follows Jesus's advice. He focuses on Jesus. He breathes deep. And he discovers that Jesus is right. All is calm again. His boat is intact, and he is not sinking. But Jesus wants to take Mack further. "Now, let's get you out of that boat," Jesus says, offering His hand.

What comes next reminds us strongly of the account of Jesus walking on the water in Matthew 14. Go ahead and read it.

> Immediately Jesus made the disciples get into the boat and go on ahead of him to the other side, while he dismissed the crowd. After he had dismissed them, he went up on a mountainside by himself to pray. Later that night, he was there alone, and the boat was already a considerable distance from land, buffeted by the waves because the wind was against it.
>
> Shortly before dawn Jesus went out to them, walking on the lake. When the disciples saw him walking on the lake, they were terrified. "It's a ghost," they said, and cried out in fear.

But Jesus immediately said to them: "Take courage! It is I. Don't be afraid."

"Lord, if it's you," Peter replied, "tell me to come to you on the water."

"Come," he said.

Then Peter got down out of the boat, walked on the water and came toward Jesus. But when he saw the wind, he was afraid and, beginning to sink, cried out, "Lord, save me!"

Immediately Jesus reached out his hand and caught him. "You of little faith," he said, "why did you doubt?"

And when they climbed into the boat, the wind died down. Then those who

"I CAN ACTUALLY DO THESE THINGS IN MY OWN LIFE. I CAN ACTUALLY START TO FORGIVE PEOPLE I DON'T LIKE. AND I CAN ACTUALLY FIND AN EASE AND A BREATH AND A CALM IN MY OWN LIFE TO GO FORWARD. THAT'S EXTREMELY RARE . . . THAT TO ME IS GREAT FILMMAKING."
—SAM WORTHINGTON, WHO PLAYS MACK

were in the boat worshiped him, saying, "Truly you are the Son of God." (verses 22–33)

What's similar about this event and Mack's experience on the lake?

How do the storms differ? Is one any less real to those experiencing it?

What is Mack's walk on the water all about? What do you think is its most important element?

> "DON'T THINK ABOUT THE PAST.
> DON'T THINK ABOUT THE PAIN.
> LOOK AT ME. EVERYTHING IS GOING
> TO BE OKAY. LOOK AT ME. TRUST ME,
> NONE OF THIS CAN HURT YOU. JUST
> KEEP YOUR EYES ON ME. BREATHE . . .
> I'M NOT GOING ANYWHERE."
> —JESUS

Seeing Jesus walking on water in real life would be an amazing, miraculous experience in and of itself. Gliding across the surface of liquid ourselves would be absolutely incredible. But what can we take away from the movie scene and Scripture passage for our everyday lives? After all, we don't often find ourselves in a boat with Jesus walking toward us on the water.

Consider these quotes by Jesus in the movie:

"Just keep your eyes on Me. Breathe."

"I'm not going anywhere."

"I'm not joking. You can do this."

"Not on your own you can't."

"You are imagining a future without Me,
and that future does not exist."

"I promised to go with you always, right?
And I'm right here."

What jumps out at you about these words? What is
the underlying message? What Bible verses do these
quotes bring to mind for you?

Whatever God is calling us to, He is always calling
us to Himself. Relationship lies at His essence as a
Trinity, and relationship with Him is the heart of how
we are meant to live this life.

In this portion of *The Shack*, Jesus calls Mack to
an extraordinary experience. Why? For the coolness
or fun of it? (Though what a fun, cool experience we
see them have!) No, it seems that relationship is what
underlies the experience. Mack is correct when he
tells Jesus, "I can't." Jesus concurs, "On your own you
can't." But Jesus wants to show Mack the reality they
can experience together.

In the same way, relationship is where and how we can realize the truth and power and practicality of God's promises to us. In the face of the brokenness that surrounds us, in spite of our pain and suffering and problems, we can know God's heart. We can move in rhythm to its beat. We can focus our eyes on Him and take our cues from His Word. And as we do, we find that He gives us what we need to calm and to heal, but also to move forward and beyond to new heights and depths.

"GOD IS OUR REFUGE AND STRENGTH, AN EVER-PRESENT HELP IN TROUBLE. THEREFORE WE WILL NOT FEAR, THOUGH THE EARTH GIVE WAY AND THE MOUNTAINS FALL INTO THE HEART OF THE SEA, THOUGH ITS WATERS ROAR AND FOAM AND THE MOUNTAINS QUAKE WITH THEIR SURGING."

—PSALM 46:1–3

ABIDE

God, thank you that you calm the storms in and around us. Thank you that you want to draw us into the supernatural experience of living and breathing with you. Give us the courage we need to fix our eyes on you and take a step of faith as we trust you. Thank you that we can rest in the knowledge that you have already conquered sin and death and that your power is made perfect in our weakness. Let us experience the power of relationship with you in the midst of our greatest storms and struggles.

TAKE IT WITH YOU

What step is God reaching out to draw you into? How will you respond this week?

PRACTICE

Message of the Week: "Keep your eyes on Me."

Memorize and Meditate: Focusing on God's Word is an excellent way to keep our eyes on Jesus in the midst of a storm. God's Word reminds us of His promises and assures us that He can be trusted. And while reading Scripture is helpful, committing verses to memory allows us to recall them quickly and meditate on them anytime and anywhere difficult or unexpected situations arise.

This week, memorize Psalm 56:3: "When I am afraid, I put my trust in you." Practice saying the verse out loud or repeating it mentally while taking deep breaths. Along with it, repeat Jesus's message to yourself: "Keep your eyes on Me." Find someone who is willing to hold you accountable to memorizing this verse and more. Share your stories with each other of times when having God's Word committed to memory helped you focus on Jesus and trust His promises through difficult times.

HOW CAN I KNOW THE HEART OF THE FATHER?

FOCUS

"For God so loved the world that he gave his one and only Son, that whoever believes in him shall not perish but have eternal life. For God did not send his Son into the world to condemn the world, but to save the world through him." —John 3:16–17

WATCH

Setup: Jesus has sent Mack up a trail to a mountain. Mack finds himself in a cavernous room, and there he encounters a beautiful woman waiting for him. She is Sophia—wisdom. Mack does not understand why he is here. Sophia tells him, "You are here for judgment." But there is a surprising twist for Mack. "Today, you are the judge," she says. He is reluctant at first, but Mack gets on a roll with a little prompting. Murderers, terrorists, abusers, his own father— they are all worthy of judgment. But being the judge is not as easy as it looks.

 Watch Video 4: Judgment

> "I DON'T WANT TO BE
> THE JUDGE ANYMORE."
> —MACK

DISCUSS

Beyond Blame

What is Mack most afraid of when he thinks he will be judged? What is he hiding from his past?

What kind of snap judgments do we make about people every day?

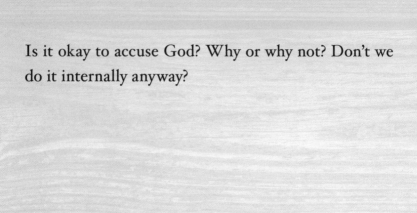

Is it okay to accuse God? Why or why not? Don't we do it internally anyway?

Would you like to have the chance to be judge? Why or why not?

Would you have judged things any differently than Mack? In what ways?

Like Mack, many of us have spent a lifetime judging others and placing blame for the hurt in our lives. Sometimes it's easier to blame others, God, and even ourselves for the pain we experience than to deal with the root of that pain. Maybe our own sense of guilt drives us to want to accuse others in order to justify ourselves. Judgment can bring a sense of power and even security, but it only compounds our pain rather than removing it.

The role of judge is not ours. The Bible tells us that job belongs to God alone: "There is only one Lawgiver and Judge, the one who is able to save and destroy. But you—who are you to judge your neighbor?" (James 4:12).

But how do we view God as judge? Too many of us see God as a vindictive enforcer, eagerly waiting for us to step out of line so He can blast us with gleeful fury. As we discussed earlier in Lesson 1, it's too easy for us to separate the character of God and view what happened on the cross as the brutal Father pounding mercilessly on the innocent Son.

Do you remember the story of Multnomah Falls that Mack told Missy? It was about an Indian tribe that was being devastated by a terrible illness. The chiefs and elders met to try to figure out how to stop this plague from wiping out their tribe. The chief knew of an old prophecy: The illness would be stopped if the daughter of a chief gave up her life for her people. But this was too great a price, and they would not ask anyone to go that far.

However, the chief's daughter heard about the prophecy and knew what she must do. She loved her tribe so much that she climbed high up to a cliff's edge—and jumped. Great healing came quickly to the tribe, but the chief was heartbroken. His tears flowed, and he cried out to the Great Spirit in anguish, asking for her death to be remembered. The Great Spirit was moved, and as the chief's tears flowed, water began to pour from the rocks, cascading down into a beautiful waterfall that flows in her memory.

Missy later brings up the Indian princess story again, asking Mack, "Why is he so mean?" How does her question and perspective capture our fear and misunderstanding of God?

> "THE LORD IS GRACIOUS AND COMPASSIONATE, SLOW TO ANGER AND RICH IN LOVE."
> —PSALM 145:8

As Mack passes judgments, Sophia traces his logic back through history, asking, "What about God? Isn't He at fault? He set all this in motion, especially if He knew the outcome." Do you agree with Mack that God is to blame? Why or why not?

How do you view God as judge? Why?

Grace in Action

By definition, grace is a free and undeserved gift. None of us can earn it, and yet God offers it to us in love. Salvation through grace is the whole reason God sent His Son, Jesus, into the world: "For God so loved the world that he gave his one and only Son, that whoever believes in him shall not perish but have eternal life. For God did not send his Son into the world to condemn the world, but to save the world through him" (John 3:16–17).

We like the idea of grace instead of judgment most of the time—at least when it applies to us. But it's easy to get hung up, like Mack does, when we start looking at who deserves grace and who doesn't. Although we don't want to be judged, we like the idea of justice and fairness. We want evil people to get what they deserve. And we want to be sure we get the good things we've been promised. In a world still marked by sin and evil, we need God's grace—and we need to trust His grace not only for ourselves but for the rest of the world as well. It's not always easy, is it?

Jesus presents us with a different perspective. His words spell out a different vision: "I and the Father are one," He said in John 10:30. "Anyone who has seen me has seen the Father," He said in John 14:9. And His actions reveal tangible examples of God's nature—complete, whole, united, Triune. Jesus reveals a deeper view of the heart of the Father.

Even with the power and authority to judge, Jesus extends God's love and grace over judgment. John 8 gives us a beautiful example of this when Jesus encountered a woman caught in adultery. The religious people of the day wanted to judge and stone her to death, and they wanted to trap Jesus by forcing Him to pass judgment. Instead, Jesus said, "Let any one of you who is without sin be the first to throw a stone at her" (verse 7). When they all turned to leave, none able to cast a stone, Jesus told the woman that He did not condemn her either.

We, too, must let go of blame by dropping the rock that we figuratively hold—but how do we reach that point? How do we grasp the grace that we've been given and extend it willingly to others, even those who have hurt us? How do we understand and feel the power of this gift that shifts the nature of our being?

We must connect with the Father's heart.

Do terrorists, abusers, murderers, and the like deserve judgment? Would you judge Missy's killer?

Who is to blame for all the pain and suffering in the world? Where does the trail of blame end?

Who are you holding captive in judgment? What step can you take to put down your stone?

Connecting with God's Heart

Mack has judged God's love and found it lacking, so Sophia presents him a final choice. He must choose which of his children will spend eternity in heaven and which will spend eternity in hell. Mack is taken aback, but Sophia explains she is only asking him to do "something that you believe God does." Sophia plays Mack's love for each child against the other as she pushes him to make a choice.

Mack begs Sophia to make this process stop, desperately promising that he'll do anything. This is an impossible choice. He loves each of his children too much. And that is what drives him to a breakthrough. "Take me instead," he cries.

Finally, Sophia is satisfied that Mack understands. He has judged his children worthy of love, even if it costs him everything. He has put himself in their place. He has willingly taken their place. He has experienced Papa's heart of love firsthand.

Read and discuss these verses from the Bible. What do they reveal about the Heavenly Father's heart?

> But because of his great love for us, God, who is rich in mercy, made us alive with Christ even when we were dead in transgressions—it is by grace you have been saved. (Ephesians 2:4–5)

> As a father has compassion on his children,
>   so the LORD has compassion on those
>   who fear him. (Psalm 103:13)

> Dear friends, never take revenge. Leave that to the righteous anger of God. For the Scriptures say,
>
> > "I will take revenge;
> >   I will pay them back,"
> >   says the LORD. (Romans 12:19, NLT)

> Let us then approach God's throne of grace with confidence, so that we may receive mercy and find grace to help us in our time of need. (Hebrews 4:16)

> The LORD is gracious and compassionate,
>   slow to anger and rich in love.
>   (Psalm 145:8)

The Lord is not slow in keeping his promise, as some understand slowness. Instead he is patient with you, not wanting anyone to perish, but everyone to come to repentance. (2 Peter 3:9)

Greater love has no one than this: to lay down one's life for one's friends. (John 15:13)

ABIDE

God, thank you that your heart is good and full of love. Thank you for the transforming gift of grace through Jesus. We don't deserve it, but we accept it as we trust in you. Please help us not only to accept your grace but to generously extend it to others, even those we struggle with. Draw us into your heart. Fill us with thankfulness, gratitude, and grace toward all we come in contact with.

TAKE IT WITH YOU

What are you blaming God for? How will confidence in the Father's heart of love change your attitude and actions this week?

PRACTICE

Message of the Week: "I'm not asking you to excuse what he's done. I'm asking you to trust Me to do what's right and to know what's best."

Gift of Grace: Who do you have a hard time loving? What person do you not want to forgive? It may be an individual person or someone who represents a group that you have judged. This week, take a step to surrender your judgment and extend grace to that person. Say or write this message and insert the person's name: "I'm not asking you to excuse what [he's] done. I'm asking you to trust Me to do what's right and to know what's best."

Your step will be specific to your situation and relationship. It may be writing a letter, making a phone call, sending flowers, delivering a meal, inviting someone to coffee or to play ball. It doesn't have to be the beginning of a close relationship, but it should be a tangible expression of the gift of grace. Decide what is appropriate, share your plan with another person in your study group, then put your plan into action this week.

"IF THERE'S HOPE FOR US AS A HUMAN RACE, WE'VE GOT TO GET PAST THE WAYS THAT WE DIVIDE OURSELVES INTO US AND THEM, AND REALIZE THAT WE'RE ALL US AND THEM INSIDE THE EMBRACE OF RELENTLESS AFFECTION."

—PAUL YOUNG, AUTHOR OF *THE SHACK*

LESSON 5

SO YOU JUST LET HIM GET AWAY WITH IT?

FOCUS

"Forgive, and you will be forgiven. Give, and it will be given to you. A good measure, pressed down, shaken together and running over, will be poured into your lap. For with the measure you use, it will be measured to you." —Luke 6:37–38

WATCH

Setup: Mack has previously encountered his own human father and experienced a deep forgiveness. Waking to a new day, he finds Papa is in the form of an older man. "For what we've got to do this morning, you're going to need a Father," Papa tells him. Papa then guides him on a strenuous hike into the woods. When Papa says, "We're here to do something that is going to be very painful for you," Mack immediately knows what's coming. He understands that Papa wants him to forgive the man who killed his daughter. He pleads, but Papa tells him that it is the path to healing for Mack. "We're on a healing trail to bring closure to this part of your journey," Papa says.

 Watch Video 5: Healing Trail

DISCUSS

On the Healing Trail

What moment do you most relate to as Mack must choose to forgive his daughter's killer?

Have you ever had to forgive someone of a terrible wrong? If so, describe what happened.

What do you think would have happened if Mack had chosen not to take a step of forgiveness?

Does Missy's killer get off the hook? What does Papa say about it?

Read and discuss the following Bible verses. How do they make you feel?

> Do not be deceived: God cannot be mocked. A man reaps what he sows. (Galatians 6:7)

> Do not take revenge, my dear friends, but leave room for God's wrath, for it is written: "It is mine to avenge; I will repay," says the Lord. On the contrary:
>
> > "If your enemy is hungry, feed him;
> > if he is thirsty, give him something to drink.
> > In doing this, you will heap burning coals on his head."
>
> Do not be overcome by evil, but overcome evil with good. (Romans 12:19–21)

What does Papa mean when He says, "You're not stuck because you *can't*. You're stuck because you *won't*"?

How is this a choice between justice and mercy?

This is the toughest challenge: Forgive the killer. Jesus said, "Love your enemies" (Matthew 5:44). But like Mack, we want them to hurt for what they did. We want God to hurt them. But it doesn't work that way. Our unforgiveness is like us drinking poison, hoping that it hurts the other guy. In reality, we are the ones who suffer from it. We all are faced with a choice. We can demand justice, holding onto our blame. Or we can choose mercy and the path to forgiveness.

The reality is that what we choose will come back to us. Here's how Jesus described it: "Forgive, and you will be forgiven. Give, and it will be given to you. A good measure, pressed down, shaken together and running over, will be poured into your lap. For with the measure you use, it will be measured to you" (Luke 6:37–38).

None of us wants to see our own guilt, but in eternal reality, we are all guilty and we all deserve separation from God. In Romans 3:23, Paul said, "For all have sinned and fall short of the glory of God." Problems arise because we want mercy for ourselves—but not for the other guy who has done us wrong. We want them to burn in hell, but we don't want to.

Fortunately, God has a bigger view. God is righteous, and He judges fairly. He can do it no other way. He doesn't play favorites, and He doesn't overlook sin and evil. Everything has consequences, and no one gets away with anything. But God loves because it's His nature. That means He loves each and every one of us equally, and as 2 Peter 3:9 says, He wants all of us to be restored to Himself: "The Lord is not slow in keeping his promise, as some understand slowness. Instead he is patient with you, not wanting anyone to perish, but everyone to come to repentance."

Forgiveness is where justice and mercy kiss. That's true when we experience forgiveness from God; it's also true when we choose to forgive others.

> "SO DO NOT FEAR, FOR I AM WITH YOU; DO NOT BE DISMAYED, FOR I AM YOUR GOD. I WILL STRENGTHEN YOU AND HELP YOU; I WILL UPHOLD YOU WITH MY RIGHTEOUS RIGHT HAND."
> —ISAIAH 41:10

Trust Me

Is forgiveness a one-time decision? Why or why not?

Is there a path to healing that bypasses forgiveness? Why or why not?

Papa says, "Forgiveness doesn't establish a relationship. It's just about letting go of his throat." What does He mean? How does this apply to real life?

Mack wants to know, "And then what?" What is Papa's answer, and how does it apply to us?

What does Papa say Mack's pain is doing to him?

From listening to Papa's words, what does He say is Mack's true choice?

Read and discuss the following Bible verses. What insights, challenges, or encouragement do they give you about forgiveness?

> Bear with each other and forgive one another if any of you has a grievance against someone. Forgive as the Lord forgave you. (Colossians 3:13)

> For if you forgive other people when they sin against you, your heavenly Father will also forgive you. But if you do not forgive others their sins, your Father will not forgive your sins. (Matthew 6:14–15)

"SON, WE'RE ON A HEALING TRAIL TO BRING CLOSURE TO THIS PART OF YOUR JOURNEY."
—PAPA

Then Peter came to Jesus and asked, "Lord, how many times shall I forgive my brother or sister who sins against me? Up to seven times?"

Jesus answered, "I tell you, not seven times, but seventy-seven times." (Matthew 18:21–22)

Two other men, both criminals, were also led out with him to be executed. When they came to the place called the Skull, they crucified him there, along with the criminals—one on his right, the other on his left. Jesus said, "Father, forgive them, for they do not know what they are doing." And they divided up his clothes by casting lots. (Luke 23:32–34)

Forgiveness can be a difficult step to take, whether the slight is minor or the crime is grievous. Like Mack, we want to hold on to the power to judge; we want to condemn. But as we discussed in our last lesson, that's not a role we hold or a power we can possess. To try is to poison ourselves.

Papa tells Mack, "I'm not asking you to excuse what he did. I'm asking you to trust Me to do what's right and to know what's best."

Isn't that what it all comes down to for us, too? Can we trust that God knows best? Can we trust that He will do what's right? Will we believe that He is the righteous judge He says He is? Can we believe that His love is enough for us? Enough to heal our hurt? Enough to apply His justice and mercy in their true and good measures?

The answer lies within our view and experience with God. If we have tasted and seen that the Lord is good (Psalm 34:8), we can fall back on our experience to believe Him. If we have encountered the heart of the Father, we can draw from the fullness He has poured into our hearts. We can allow our heartbeat to align with His. We can follow His leading to let go of the throats of those who have hurt and wronged us.

Forgiveness can be a long process, especially for deep wounds. But we can start by simply saying it. It won't be the only time; we usually have to repeat it often over time. As Papa notes in the movie, forgiveness doesn't have to establish a relationship—we don't have to be best buddies with the other person—but it must be genuine to release its hold.

In Mack's case, he didn't know the perpetrator of the crime. We might be in a similar situation, but we might also know those who have hurt us. We may see them on a regular basis, even if we try to avoid them. God has called us to join Him in the work of reconcil-

> ## "YOU DON'T HAVE TO DO THIS ALONE. I'M HERE WITH YOU."
> —PAPA

iation, and part of that may be restoring relationships in our lives with people who have hurt us. The apostle Paul said it like this: "Bear with each other and forgive one another if any of you has a grievance against someone. Forgive as the Lord forgave you" (Colossians 3:13).

But that might be a long way off. It may come with time as God works and heals. What's most important now is simply focusing on the first step: letting go of their throat, releasing our hold on our blame and bitterness. And letting God draw us to Himself, where we can find the strength to cling to and act on His words: "You don't have to do this alone. I'm here with you."

As we continue to choose forgiveness, the path gets easier as we find freedom from the grip of bitterness.

God with Us

What finally gives Mack the strength to forgive?

If God is always with us, why does the Bible tell us to seek Him? What does it promise when we do?

How can we tap into and experience God's presence?

What other ways throughout *The Shack* do we see Papa, Jesus, and Sarayu providing their presence to Mack?

How can forgiving others help draw you even closer into the presence of God?

How does forgiveness begin for Mack? How does it begin now for you?

Our God is a God of presence. Not just omnipresent in a vague sort of way, He is *with us*—real, personal, close. He cares about the moments of our lives. Jesus said He knows the number of hairs on our heads (Luke 12:7). Psalm 139 paints a beautiful picture of God's intimate knowledge of us from before birth:

> Where can I go from your Spirit?
>> Where can I flee from your presence?
> If I go up to the heavens, you are there;
>> if I make my bed in the depths, you
>> are there.
> If I rise on the wings of the dawn,
>> if I settle on the far side of the sea,
> even there your hand will guide me,
>> your right hand will hold me fast.
>> (verses 7–10)

It's no coincidence that Jesus is called Immanuel, "God with us." This name was prophesied about Him centuries before He came to earth. Its importance can't be understated. When the angel appeared to Joseph to let him know about the extraordinary plan unfolding around him, the angel used the name Immanuel for Jesus (Matthew 1:23).

Jesus embodies the miracle of God with us. He was God come to earth to take on human form and make a way for us to be truly reunited with our Heavenly Father. But His presence remains with us. While He was physically here on earth, He promised, "And I will ask the Father, and he will give you another advocate to help you and be with you forever—the Spirit of truth. The world cannot accept him, because it neither sees him nor knows him. But you know him, for he lives with you and will be in you. I will not leave you as orphans; I will come to you" (John 14:16–18).

In *The Shack,* God knows exactly what Mack is facing during the most difficult part of his journey—and God is by his side with this promise: "You don't have to do this alone. I'm here with you." God gives us the same promise. We don't have to forgive alone. We don't have to do life alone. God is still here—with us.

ABIDE

God, thank you that you are always with us—not just somewhere nearby, but right here with us, loving and guiding us through each day. Help us to forgive as you have forgiven us. Please fill us with your love to fuel our ability to let go of the throats of those who do us wrong. Thank you that you will continue to journey with each one of us as we learn to trust you to do what's right and know what's best.

TAKE IT WITH YOU

Who do you need to choose to forgive? What is your first step on that journey?

"WHEN I TAKE ON A CHARACTER, I TRY TO BE AS TRUTHFUL AS POSSIBLE. ACTING IS JUST TRUTH IN IMAGINARY SITUATIONS. AND THIS IS ABSOLUTE TRUTH IN AN ABSOLUTE IMAGINARY SITUATION."
—SAM WORTHINGTON, WHO PLAYS MACK

PRACTICE

Message of the Week: "Forgiveness doesn't establish a relationship. It's just about letting go of his throat."

Letting Go: Who is it that has hurt you the most? Who have you struggled or refused to forgive? In Mack's case, he didn't personally know the man. That might be true for us. Or the subject of our bitterness may not be alive any longer. Or maybe they are, and you see them regularly. Whatever the circumstances, let forgiveness begin now.

Write a note or letter directed to this person. You can choose how much of your past emotions you want to pour into this message, but don't get stuck there. Turn the tide toward forgiveness. Take the step to say

you forgive this person. Spell it out specifically: "I forgive you."

Next, set an empty chair across from you. If possible, place a picture of the other person on the chair.
Read your letter out loud as if you were reading it to
that person.

When you are done, you may want to shred or burn
(in a safe spot like a fireplace) your letter in a symbolic
gesture of releasing your grudge. If the person is someone you know, you might want to tell them directly
in another note or in person that you have chosen to
forgive them. However you follow up, choose today to
take the step of forgiveness and say, "I forgive you."